Thy Kingdom First

"About My Father's Business"

Created By:

Luther T. Collins

Printed in the United States of America by
Ingram Spark
www.ingramspark.com

© Copyright 2020 by Luther T. Collins

All rights reserved. This book or parts thereof may not be reproduced in any form, stored in a retrieval system, or transmitted in any form by any means- electronic, mechanical, photocopy, recording, or otherwise-without prior written permission of the author, except as provided by United States of America copyright law.

Scripture references are taken from the King James Version, and other versions of the Holy Bible.

Cover Design by Vince White
Spine & Book Sizing by Chris Kitt Jr.

ISBN: 978-1-7351253-1-2

To contact author for booking or additional copies, go to: luthertcollins0408@gmail.com

Thy Kingdom First

"About My Father's Business"

Created By:

Luther T. Collins

When I knock on your door, won't you answer me?
When I call on your name, will you show thyself approved?
What will your legacy say about you?
Were you here on this earth for a purpose?
Who are you really, and why did you come?
Who sent you, and where's your daddy?

O taste and see just how good the Lord can be.
O give thanks unto the Lord for he is good and his mercy endures forever.
Hear my voice for I am the Alpha, the Omega, the first and the last.
Before me there was none, and after me there will be none.
Only if you call upon my name will I hear you, and then I shall answer.
I have given you the ability to speak those things that be not as though they were for such a time as this.

My sheep know my voice.
The joy of the Lord is your strength.

Special Celebrations

First and foremost, I celebrate my Lord and Savior, Jesus Christ, for without him I am nothing. From the dust I was created, and from the dust I shall one day return. God graced me with this unique gift and ability to write, inspire, lead, and motivate a dying world for such a time as this. Thank you, God for taking a broken individual like myself and making me into a mighty, wisdom-filled, and power-packed man of God. If he did it for me, surely he can do it for you.

I celebrate my beautiful wife, LaTasha Collins, for being my rock. I honor you and truly value what we have built over the years. You are awesome, amazing, extravagant, outstanding, and all together lovely. Thank you for your patience during the process and your unconditional love throughout every test and trial. It takes a special woman to love someone like me, and you my dear are that special woman. You are my queen and my world as the best is truly yet to come for you.

To my children who I won't list for specific personal reasons that I won't disclose at this time. When I wrote this book in 2016 my youngest had not yet arrived, welcome to the tribe my boy. See, I listened to God, as this was the only thing I listened to in the Bible at the time, when God said, "Be fruitful and multiply." Each of my children holds a special place in my heart. There is no such thing as a stepchild, although this could be one of the toughest relationships that you experience in life outside of marriage based on circumstances, as they go hand in hand. I love you all unconditionally and will do my best to be the best dad ever in the years to come.

In the bible, it says honor your parents so that you may have a long life. My modified version of this is leave your parents to join your spouse, but don't let them go and never stop listening to them, for their wisdom births life into your destiny. Thank you mom, Gail C. Harris, for loving me through thick and thin! You had my back even when I was stubborn and would not listen to your advice. You loved me through pain, through agony, through defeat, and through death. You never gave up on me and you never left me down when I fell. Parenting never came with a handbook or guide but you always did the best you could with what you had especially with my biological father never being in the picture as a positive presence.

I celebrate my spiritual parents Apostle Travis and Pastor Stephanie Jennings of Harvest Tabernacle in Lithonia, GA. I thank you for the impartation and amazing example you set daily. You are awesome leaders and I thank God for your leadership and guidance.

I also have to say a special thank you to Apostle Vanessa C. Thomas (Behind the Veil Christian Ministries, Richmond, VA), Bishop Darren L. Gay Sr. (Higher Way Ministries, Petersburg, VA), Pastor James T. Elam Jr. (Dunamis Christian Center, Newport News, VA), and Pastor Yolanda Scott (New Life Ministries, Petersburg, VA).

To my family, Collins and Valentine, thank you for those who have supported me along the way. All my aunts and uncles who helped raise me, Joyce and John White, Dorthy Parker, Vonnie and Van Harris, Margaret and Frank Griggs, Randy and Kathy Collins, Kelvin and Shirl Collins, Bubba Collins, Amelia and James Humphrey, Jewel Tyree, and the list goes on. I'm thankful for each and every cousin, sister, brother (Dr. Lamar T. Collins Sr.), niece, nephew, and relative in my family. I can't forget about some of the many late greats that make us so unique as a family, such as Eula and Bill Kennedy, Virginia and Buddy Tyree, Brenda Ford, Masquai White, Jerome (Hog) Tyree, Robert McSwain, William Harris, Margaret Valentine-Collins, Luther Collins, and the list goes on. I love you all, as you all have and always will hold a very special place in my heart. Family inspires and uplifts during happy and sad times. Family makes life easy when times are hard most of the time (LOL).

What is a man with no friends? I don't have many as it's safer that way, but I thank those near and dear to my heart as I will only name a few. Vince White, one of the baddest graphics design guys in the land, our friendship is very unique, as we have been boys since day one. From performances to you designing clothing and book covers for me, the history is real. Ernest Jackson and Chris Kitt Jr., you are both my brothers from another mother who have been there through thick and thin.

Thank you to my mentors and family friends Dr. Tony Williams, Mr. David Banks, Mr. Charles (Anne McLaurin) Meeker, Robbie (Marlowe) Carruth, Wayne Brown, and the list goes on. Brother Nick Jones, I can't leave you out. You are like a big brother, mentor, and wise counselor to me all in one. I thank you for helping me during a very tough transition of my life, as God knows who to put in your corner.

I thank all of my coworkers, friends and family not listed, and to all who have purchased my book. I am excited about this one, as I know you will truly be inspired and uplifted. This is the first of many things God has graced me to do in this historic year. I'm looking for historic book sales so please tell somebody that knows somebody that knows somebody to pick up a copy today.

I am so grateful for everything and love you all as I leave light and life with you in *Thy Kingdom First "About My Father's Business."* And yes, there will be more-best sellers to follow.

Contents

Chapter 1: Salvation is Everything

Chapter 2: Write the Vision and Make it Plain

Chapter 3: Grace and Mercy

Chapter 4: The Time is Now

Chapter 5: Revelation and Destination

Chapter 6: Covering

Chapter 7: Create in Me a Clean Heart

Chapter 8: Creative Arts

Chapter One
Salvation Is Everything

Without God we are nothing, as it is him that gives us the ability to walk, talk, think, breathe, and use our limbs everyday in this journey called life. We often take this for granted but know and understand that there is always someone who is worse off than you. For example, when you can't pay your rent or can't put food on the table, we never think about that man or woman on the street who holds that sign because his or her family is truly homeless. We never take the time to go to shelters and talk to those individuals who were once in our shoes and everything spiraled downhill leaving them with nothing. We never take the time to look at that man or woman who was born with a birth defect that may never be normal, because we only see ourselves, which equates to selfishness.

We have to transform that selfishness into selflessness. We have the best example in our Father who is in heaven for he is love. For God so loved the world (you and me) that he gave his only begotten son that whosoever believes in him shall not perish but have everlasting life (John 3:16). Can you honestly say that you would give your child for someone else? That's what God did; he loved us that much even when we didn't deserve it. Ask yourself this: When you should have died, why didn't you? We've all had those experiences, whether we missed a bullet or purposely put ourselves in a dangerous situation. Who was it that truly got us through that tough circumstance or situation? It's funny because even atheists call on the name of the Lord when they are in trouble. Just remember, if you deny God, he will deny you. Can you honestly say that you're the reason for your own existence? If so, you're clearly in denial.

Let's go back to John 3:16 in the latter part of the scripture which is the most important, "That whosoever believes in him shall not perish but have everlasting life." That itself is a blessing as it gives life to every individual walking the face of this earth. This clearly represents what you must do in order to receive salvation. It's telling you how you can live and not die, but first you must believe in our Father who is in heaven, whom you can't see but who sees everything. There's another scripture that states if you confess with your mouth and believe in your heart that Jesus is Lord, you shall be saved.

Please understand nothing else matters on this earth, as there is nothing more important than your salvation. Your salvation is your livelihood and represents life. God came so that we may have life and have it more abundantly. Who is it that is on the edge and has not received this gift of salvation? Salvation costs nothing, yet its value cannot be measured in riches and gold. Meaning you can have all the money in the world and all the possessions of the earth, but if you don't have God, than you truly have nothing. As one of my Pastors/Spiritual Fathers (Pastor James T. Elam Jr. of Dunamis Christian Center, Newport

News, VA) used to say, "What in hell do you want?" You have to ask yourself that question if you choose to reject salvation.

Man does not have a heaven or hell to put you in, as we don't answer to man, but to God. When you leave this earth, you have to return your rental suit/body, and you can't take any of your earthly possessions with you. This is something to think about as life comes and goes, and it's a pretty fast process. If you think back to when you were young, you said, "I can't wait till I'm fourteen so I can work," "I can't wait till I'm sixteen so I can drive," "I can't wait till I'm eighteen so I can be grown," "I can't wait till I'm twenty-one so I can drink or be legal." Don't lie; some of us used to say this, as I know I did. After twenty-one we don't wish or request to be older much after this; it just happens. Although you do get those who want to be twenty-five so they can get into the grown and sexy clubs (LOL). But if you noticed, after this the time flies by, as nobody says, "I can't wait to be thirty," "I can't wait to be forty," "I can't wait to be fifty," "I can't wait to be one hundred."

Life may seem long at times but it is truly much shorter than we think. That's why it's so important not to take life for granted and understand that life is a gift from God. The good news for us is that if you are still breathing, you still have an opportunity to receive this free gift of salvation. We never know when we will take our last breath, so we must not take this opportunity lightly. If a grocery store said they were going to give out free food for an entire day, everyone and their mom would be there getting free food. If a gas station said they were giving out free gas, especially when the gas prices are elevated, everyone and their mama would be there too getting free gas. So why is it that we won't take this free gift of salvation?

We don't embrace or won't receive what we don't understand. On this earth we will all have the opportunity to receive salvation before making our final departure. Some invitations will come in different shapes and forms, but the opportunity will always be there. Some may go to church, some may be witnessed to, some may hear from God, and the list goes on. The question is, when your time comes, will you be open to receive the invitation of salvation from the Lord? We have tried many things in life whether they may have been good or bad. Most of us can admit we tried drinking, we tried smoking, we tried drugs, we tried sleeping around, we tried stealing, we tried lying, we tried cheating, we tried something that we should not have, and for the rest of you, I'll cast out-lying demons in a minute, as Pastor James T. Elam Jr. would say. The point is if we tried all these things and they did not work and could not give us joy and fulfillment to keep us, then why not try God?

Notice I had to add joy and fulfillment, because there are some of us that are still getting high on our own supply. There are still some of us that are drinking until we pass out. There are still some of us that are sleeping with everyone that is available, not knowing their next victim could be infected with AIDS but won't tell because they want it just as bad as you do. Looks can be deceiving and everything that looks good is not always good, as I'm sure you have realized this by now. If not, just keep living, and you will soon see.

For those of you living who are seeking salvation and don't know how to be saved, it's as simple as this. You have to acknowledge your sins by asking for forgiveness and asking God to come into your heart after asking for forgiveness, as God will not dwell in an unclean temple or in a dirty person. It's just like when you wake up in the morning or go to bed at night. If you don't take a shower, then you are dirty, and if you are dirty, then not too many people will want to deal with you, let alone be around you. Our father is the same way; if you are full of evil (dirty) or have a sinful nature with no repentance, then God will not come into your heart.

You cannot serve two masters, as you have to ask yourself, what are you putting (serving) before God? Is it your money that you are serving and worshipping? Is it other gods, as our God is a jealous God and will not play second to anyone? Just remember that money cometh and money goeth and other gods don't have a heaven or hell to place you in. The same way we grow up from a toddler or baby to different phases and stages in life, we must also grow up in God. We can't stay on breast milk forever just like we can't crawl and be carried forever. At some point we have to stand up on our own two feet and begin to walk on our own. This is a part of life as we grow and we become wiser with time by learning from others as well as our own mistakes.

You have to prioritize and get your life in order for things to flow right in your life. Write this down over and over, as this is your key to success in life as your priorities should always be God, family, and work. Once you get your priorities in line, then everything else will work out for the greater good in your life. With that being said, don't get it twisted. You will still have tests and trials in life, but God said, "There is no test or trial that is not common to man." What this means is there is nothing you can face on this earth that somebody else has not faced and whipped prior to your crisis. Don't ever think you are the only person who has contemplated suicide. Don't think you are the only person who has ever been raped. Don't think you are the only person who has been abused. Don't think you are the only person who has been cheated on. Don't think you are the only person who has ever been broken. Don't think. Don't think. Don't think.

Believe it or not, there is a saying that your mom or dad would always say that still holds true until today. There is nothing you can do that I haven't already done, as this is still a very true statement on today. Yes, times are different, but it's still already been done just in a different format. Maybe back in the days when mom and dad skipped school, they had to catch a bus or walk if cars weren't readily available in those days (LOL). Back in the days mom and dad may have smoked a little weed;

only difference they didn't have all the flavors they have now, and they couldn't pick and choose from the different varieties of wrapping papers of today. Back in the day mom and dad used to be the life of the party, but they ain't gone tell you about it. Back in the day mom and dad used to sleep around and had a reputation for it, but they ain't gone tell you about that either. So when we say, naw, they couldn't possibly know in reality, they do, but they just don't want to tell you or even think about that.

We all got some "ain't gone tell you" stuff that we buried in our minds, but guess what, by grace we have been forgiven, and that's the beauty of salvation. All that bad stuff we did, God forgave us for this when we received him in our hearts. Now with that being said, I'm hopeful that we changed our ways, as you shouldn't have to repent continuously for the same thing every week, as there has to be a desire to change. Salvation saves you from a hopeless, endless life that will take you on the road of nowhere fast. God is the way, the truth, and the light, and through him you can live life to the fullest until your cup overfloweth.

First you must confess, then you must believe, and then you will receive salvation. It's as easy as "Forgive me, God, for my sins. I believe you died for me. I make a decision this day to make you Lord and Savior of my life. Therefore I am saved!" Say this with authority, receive God, and your life will never ever be the same. You don't have to have long, drawn-out, well-scripted, or prepared verses. It's not about that as it's all about getting right with God. I hope you have received something from this chapter, as this is the most important thing you could ever do in life in receiving this free gift of salvation. It will save your soul from a burning hell in eternity. If you don't know what hell is, turn your oven on to the highest degree and picture ten times hotter than that. That is hell, and that is where you are going to spend eternity when you pass away if you do not receive salvation.

      Let go and let God, for your life does not belong to you, and the sooner you realize this, the sooner you will live and not die. God is so good that he did not let you die in your mess, as he only wants you to get it right and have a relationship with him. Once you get into right standing with God, then he is able to fight those battles that once seemed hopeless in your life. You have tried everything else; why not try God? God will make a way, and God can make a way only if you let him. So as you go about your day and your life, remember that salvation is everything and without God we are nothing.

Chapter Two
Write the Vision and Make it Plain

Write the vision and make it plain according to what God has called you to be. In Habakkuk 2:2 it gives you clear instructions on what to do. It also states that the vision is for an appointed time. Which means that it may not happen today or tomorrow but it will surely come to pass. This doesn't mean you're writing "I want to be a millionaire" and that's your so called vision. Your vision is that thing that you like doing that you never get tired of. Your vision is that gift that God graced you to do effortlessly. Your gift is a natural flowing ability that God gives you where you excel better than others in this area. But first and foremost you have to write, as it gives you clear instructions in the scripture. If a man or woman of God speaks over your life, write it down. If God graces you to do something, write it down. Whatever your heart's desire may be, write it down as long as it lines up with God's word and will. So before you do anything, the first thing you must do is write your vision down on paper.

Everyone will not have the same vision, as everyone is not graced to do the same thing. You may be graced to work with kids, where your sister or brother may be graced to be an attorney, a doctor, a basketball player, a football player, a therapist, a writer, a musician, a meteorologist, an actor, a scientist, a politician, a preacher, a delivery driver, a business owner, etc. And the most important thing about a vision, you have to understand it's for an appointed time. If God gives us stuff too soon before the appointed time, it could affect our outcome. That's why God, who sees all and knows all, says if we wait, though it may tarry, it will surely come to pass. It also says make it (the vision) plain so that he who reads it runs. This basically means write it clearly so others will see it easily and quickly and know what God has assigned you to do. If they are not for you, then they will surely run; however, if they are for you, they will support you and back you in preparing your vision to come to pass.

Now having the vision is the start, but once you have the vision, what you do next is very critical. So we wrote the vision and made it plain; now it's time to prepare for the vision. If God told you that you were going to be a pilot for your pastor, then you have been graced to fly. This means you should be working on getting your pilot license and going to pilot school to get whatever necessary credentials you need to have to fly. You don't worry about how you're going to get a plane or what plane you will fly, as this stuff is for God to determine.

Matthew 6:25-27 states: "Therefore I say to you, do not worry about your life, what you will eat or what you will drink; nor about your body, what you will put on. Is not life more than food and the body more than clothing? Look at the birds of the air, for they neither sow nor reap nor gather into barns; yet your heavenly father feeds them. Are you not of more value than they? Which of you by worrying can add one cubit to his stature?" Now this clearly shows that you can apply this to any situation or circumstance. If you are writing the vision and making it plain, then you prepare as you wait. You don't worry, but you wait patiently and prepare. In your preparation you don't try to figure things out. You do the natural and watch God put the *super* on your *natural* as he perfects what is imperfect.

In this preparation you have to understand there will be peaks and valleys, as not every day will be ice cream and cake. There will be some challenges and some turmoil because if God is going to give you something, he has to know he can trust you. If God promised you wealth, he has to know you will tithe your 10 percent of all your first fruits and follow the principle for giving (10-10-80). If your lights get cut off today, this doesn't mean your vision will not come to pass. If you fall behind on rent or mortgage and get evicted or foreclosed on, this does not mean your vision will not come to pass.

Sometimes God has to test you before he blesses you. God needs to know that if he blesses you tomorrow, that you will still give him the glory and make the right decisions. To be honest if God blesses us at the wrong time, we will meet our destruction in most cases. This simply means if God blesses you with millions and you are still struggling with that drug addiction, what do you think will happen to those millions? And by him blessing you, he will not get the glory, and the ending is not very happy. Know that God will test you but it also says in the bible that God will not put more on us than we can bear. So if your test is hard and you are pushed to your limits, you should be celebrating simply because God has that much faith in you that he allowed you to go through that test.

Somebody else would have blown their brains out if they had to go through that bad marriage, that bankruptcy, that murder charge, that financial devastation, that month without food, that period of homelessness, that car repossession, that loss of a love one, and the list goes on. Sometimes you have to go through for the sake of someone else, but know God is molding you and shaping you while you are going through for the new season in your life. So during your preparation phase, be ready for tests and trials but understand that God has you, and if God is for you, who can be against you? In preparing you are extending or executing your faith, which basically means you are already operating as if God has done it for you in advance.

Going back to the earlier example, if you were to be the pilot for your pastor, you would start reaching out to your pastor and find out what kind of plane he or she would like. Find out who has that plane and practice flying this plane. Start envisioning the plane and where the plane will be kept. By doing this, you are walking on the word and extending your faith. In the bible it says, "Faith without works is dead", so the preparation is vital in writing the vision and making it plain. If you never do the natural, God will never do the super. If God calls you to do something and you never take the first step, then

God cannot activate your vision because you have disrupted the operation process. For we walk by faith and not by sight, for if you never walk through the darkness you'll never see the light.

After the preparation period you have to wait and not worry. Notice when you wait, it's not always comfortable or easy. A prime example is when you go to the emergency room, whether it's for you or you're coming to see a loved one. It's not an easy thing to do to wait when you don't know what the outcome will be. That's the same thing with us. We know God has a purpose and a plan, but we don't know how long the wait will be. Though it may take a while, we have to wait. Though it may not happen when we want it to, we have to wait. Though we have numerous obstacles, we have to wait. You have to understand that the enemy has peeked into your future, and he sees the marvelous and wonderful things your future holds, and for that reason he wants you to lose sight of the promise. If he can get you to turn back and go back to your evil ways, guess what, he can stop you from reaching your destiny.

Your destiny is for an appointed time and an appointed place to be predetermined by God. God knew before we were even out of our mother's womb what we would do in this life and when we would do it. So know that God has a plan and there is no failure in God. Know that the waiting process may be long and tedious, but if you just hold on a little while longer, it shall come to pass. What is it that God promised you that you are oh-so-close to breaking through? Don't throw in the towel and don't give in, as your breakthrough is just around the corner. Don't be the person who quits or walks away when the blessing is right there. Just like the song says, those who wait on the Lord, he shall renew their strength. This means God will keep you during this period of waiting.

Think about the Footprints in the Sand; when you're strengthened and you're good, you can walk on your own. But when the time comes to where you do not have the strength to walk on your own, God will carry you through. When you're battling that court case and you no longer have the strength to fight the battle, God will carry you through. When you're going up against that boss at work and you've done all that you can do, know that God will carry you through. When you don't have the money to put gas in your car and have to pray your way home, God will carry you through. When you don't have the money to put food on the table, God will carry you through. You have to trust and believe in God's perfect will for your life while you are waiting. You have to know that God has you and that every answer to every prayer is yea and amen.

With that being said, this prayer must line up to his will. For instance, God is not going to honor your prayer if you pray to win the lottery. The lottery is based on luck, and God does not operate on luck. If you win the lottery, you're going to think you did it, and you will glorify yourself and your lotto ticket. When God does something, it's never a question of luck or chance, as God does those things that we can't do on our own.

And lastly, while you are waiting, start expecting the greater good. Basically this means start walking in vision as you should be not only looking for your vision to come to pass but speaking it as well. In the bible it says, "Call (speak) those things that be not as though they were." This basically means if you want to be a doctor, start saying, "I am a doctor." By doing this you put your faith in action and hold God accountable to his word. God cannot lie, so if he says it, then that settles it, it will come to pass. If you're going to be a writer, start writing and start saying, "I am a great writer." If you're going to be a dancer, tell yourself every day, "I am a great dancer," and start dancing. As a man or woman thinketh, so is he or she, so if you think you can, then you can. If you can think it, you can believe it, and if you believe it, you can receive it. You cannot receive anything that you don't first believe that you can do. If you don't believe in yourself, you won't exert the effort to bring your vision to life.

As you can see, there is a lot of work required in bringing your vision to pass. It shall be done, it will be done, it can be done, it's already done, but it's all up to you. If you do your part and allow God to do his part, then you can receive that thing God has promised over your life. Be patient, be inspired, be humble, and be ready, as God has great things for you. Everyone has their very own special gift, and it's up to you as an individual to find out what this gift is and how to use it. If you don't know what your gift is, ask God and he will tell you. Once you have your gift, never let go of what God has given you but embrace your gift. This year is going to be historic so what better way to celebrate history than to exercise your gift and be a part of this amazing year. This year God is gracing those chosen individuals too not only walk in their gift, but to experience life like never before, as this is only for the believers and children of God. So if you have not done it yet, it's time for you to write your vision and make it plain so God can make you prosper in your vision at the appointed time.

Chapter Three
Grace and Mercy

Grace and mercy is what God gives us even when we don't deserve it. In 2 Corinthians 12:9 God says, "My grace is sufficient for you, for my strength is made perfect in weakness." This simply means God's grace is enough to get you through that touch circumstance or situation that you are facing. His grace makes us strong when we are weak and carries us when we are lacking the strength to carry on. In 1 Chronicles 16:34 it states: "Oh, give thanks to the Lord, for he is good! For his mercy endures forever." If you noticed, it says give thanks first. In everything you do, thank God for what he has already done before asking for anything else. How can God bless you with something else if you are not grateful for what he has already done? By thanking God, you acknowledge what he has done for you. His mercy is what keeps us when we need to be kept. God's mercy allows us to live when we should be dead. In addition God's mercy covers us in his blood when we do not deserve to be covered. When we do those things that are not pleasing in God's sight, it's his grace and mercy that saves us. We all have some "ain't gone tell you" stuff in our lives. That's those things we did that we are ashamed of that a lot of people don't know about but God knows.

When we repent, God forgives us and washes our sleigh clean only because of his mercy and grace. We can never forget that God sent his only begotten son, Jesus, who died so that we may have life and have it more abundantly. And instead of letting us die in our mess, God kept us for such a time as this by his grace and mercy. In taking you through, God again gives you grace to carry you over those trials and tribulations which will eventually become testimonies. Nevertheless we must be obedient and hearken to the voice of the Lord when he tells us to do something. It is a blessing that we will never know how much it cost to see our sins up on that cross. This is a true representation of grace and mercy because his death granted life for you and for me.

Another example of God's grace would be Genesis 6:8: "But Noah found grace in the eyes of the Lord." During this point in time God was not pleased with the wickedness of man and the evil thoughts of man's heart. However, God found favor in Noah and was pleased with Noah. Noah was an upright, blameless, and honest man after God's own heart. Because of grace, God spared Noah and his family when he brought about a great storm to destroy mankind. We all should know the story of Noah's Ark, as this is a true example of how God gives one grace. In this particular case Noah, being the man of God that he was, was well deserving of this grace.

However, we as individuals do not always deserve the grace that God gives us, as this is where the mercy comes in. If truth be told and we were back in the Old Testament days, we would be an extinct nation. In those days you were immediately judged by your actions, and the punishments were much harsher. When they said an eye for an eye and a tooth for a tooth, they mean it. In those days if you sinned, you could lose a limb or be stoned. In today's society if you sin, it is praised and acknowledged as a good thing in some cases. Prime example, if you stole in the Old Testament, your hands were cut off. If you steal today you can be praised by your friends who may encourage you to steal more. Being caught in today's society does not necessarily rectify the problem. Not everyone who's caught and gets punished changes their ways. How many criminals do you know that were jailed and then released only to commit the same crime? This shows there is clearly no reverence or respect for authority and most importantly God. In the Old Testament days if you had a hand cut off for stealing and decided to steal again, they probably wouldn't cut off your other hand but take your life in return.

On the back end of that grace, you have mercy, as this is what preserves your life. In today's society we take mercy for granted yet we must understand that when we were in the wrong, it was nothing but God's mercy on us that allowed us to make it through that situation. When you were drinking and driving and fell asleep behind the wheel, it was the mercy that brought you home safely. When you were sleeping around with everyone unprotected, it was the mercy that kept you from contracting AIDS. When you were hanging out in the streets in the midst of drive-bys and gun shots, it was the mercy that kept you safe.

When you were in that compromising situation, it was God's mercy that let you make it through. If we ever take the time to truly reflect on those situations, I'm sure there were many times where our lives were spared out of no control of our own. It was during this time that God covered us for such a time as this.

Sometimes in life we have to go through these obstacles and make these bad decisions in order for us to truly be in position. What I mean by this is God has called each and every one to operate in the gift which he has given us. That gift could be anything, but in order to operate in the gift, you have to have some experience under your belt in order to be effective. For example, no pastors are perfect individuals and have all had some sort of struggles in life. God knew their path long before they were ever conceived, as they had to go through the process in order to arrive to their current destination. Because if you truly look at the bigger picture, that pastor had to be delivered from some things and go through some hell in order to teach individuals like me and you how to get through those same situations. That same pastor was graced and anointed to their calling based on going through the valley and coming out as pure gold. If they did not go through that battle with sickness, prostitution, persecution, perversion, judgment, addiction, strongholds, etc., then how can they ever help someone else get delivered in that arena? If you haven't been down that road, then you can't effectively give instructions on how to get past the roadblocks on that particular street. Putting it in layman's terms, if you haven't been tested in a certain area, then you can't tell someone else how to make it out. Life is full of experiences through tests and trials. Not everyone will endure the same encounters, as this is what makes us unique. Not everyone will be gifted in the same areas, and things that one person can handle the next individual may not be able to handle.

In Hebrews 4:16 the bible says: "Let us therefore come boldly to the throne of grace that we may obtain mercy and find grace to help in time of need." In this passage it clearly states, let us go to Go with boldness in his thrown of grace. For God's grace cannot amount to any size of monetary value and is more precious than anything on this earth. Without grace, we will surely die and not live. By coming boldly to God's throne of grace, we may receive mercy and find the grace to get us out of that tough situation. By obtaining his mercy, we may live when we were supposed to die. By obtaining his mercy, we may receive favor to get through when we should have been defeated. It is God's mercy that allows us to find his grace which far passes all understanding. For we are not perfect people living in this world, and you must understand that because of God's mercy and grace, we are forgiven of our sinful ways when we ask for forgiveness.

Going back to the Old Testament, they did not have this extension of mercy and grace which made them subject to the wrath of God. Could you truly imagine if you were immediately judged for all of your actions? For instance, if you killed a person, you would be killed right then and there without question. If you robbed a person, your hand would be cut off. If you slept with someone prior to marriage, you would be killed. If you used your sight for evil, your eyes would be cut out. Could you honestly say that you could survive on this earth without grace and mercy? In the Bible it says that we have all sinned and come short of the glory of God. This basically means that at some point, as long as you keep living, you are going to make mistakes and you are going to sin whether intentional or unintentional. So instead of dying in our mess because we are not perfect, God extends his grace and mercy so that we may have life. This is unselfishness at the highest level. How many friends or family members do you have right now that if they had to choose between them dying or you dying would say, "I'll die for you?" Not very many, as this is what God did for us because of his love for us. He allowed his only son to die for us so that we could get things right and repent from our wicked ways.

  Sin comes in many shapes and forms, as it doesn't matter whether it's a big or small sin. That murderer is just as bad as that backbiter just like that adulterous is just as bad as that gossiper. At the end of the day it's all sin, and if we were to be judged on this without grace or mercy, the outcome would not be good. How long do you honestly think that you would survive on this earth without God's grace and mercy? That accident that you were supposed to die in was covered by grace. That stray bullet with your name on it was covered by grace. That death penalty that was hanging over your head was covered by grace. That situation that you thought you escaped out of that no one knew about was covered by grace. If God loves you that much that he gave you grace and mercy just to spare your life, why wouldn't you love him back in return? No amount of money or worldly possessions can come close to equaling the true value of God's grace and mercy. Through grace, God exonerates you or clears you from blame or execution. This is huge, as God uses grace to give you a clean slate when you repent for your sins so that you may have life and have it more abundantly.

Grace is a form of favor which can also be defined as clemency, forgiveness, mercifulness, or charity. It's like God saying, "I love you so much that I will give you clemency instead of the death penalty. I love you so much that I will forgive you instead of punishing you. I love you so much that I will give you charity even though you don't deserve it." That's the kind of God we serve, as there is no failure in God. Mercy can also be viewed as a form of favor just the same. God's mercy can be viewed as compassion and forbearance. God mercy says, "I'll withhold or keep back your punishment and wipe your slate clean," which is also known as forbearance. God's mercy says, "I'll be compassionate when I should not be, even when you denied or rejected me."

How many friends and family members do you have that can say the same? Can you even say the same for yourself? What about that person that wronged you and you never let them forget it? If God were to hold our sins against us, we would be in hell pleading for a drink of water. If all of our sins were openly displayed, how many people would give us a second chance? In the Bible it says, "Judge not, and ye shall not be judged." Who is it that you are judging out there when you have blemishes on your record unknown to man? If God can love us enough to show us mercy and grace when we don't deserve it, then why can't we do the same? God's mercy and grace covers a multitude of our sins, and his blood washes us clean as snow no matter how many times we fell short. So as you can see, mercy and grace give us breath daily because without them we are nonexistent.

Chapter 4
The Time Is Now

For those that didn't know, we are living in the last days. So if there was ever a time to seek God, the time is most definitely now. In this life as a Christian, we have to run the race and keep our eyes on the prize. In doing so, we can't afford to look back, and we must always take the time to locate our hindrances. When you are winning the race, you can't afford to slow down by dwelling in your past, as this has designed your future. God will let you go through so his glory can be revealed through your mess. And on the opposite side of this, when you are losing the race, you must not get discouraged by giving up and giving in. Life will always throw curveballs your way, and you will fall down, but if you don't get up, you can't continue in the race. Every day in this life will not be ice cream and cake, but every day you're breathing you have an opportunity to make things right.

Since tomorrow is not promised, the time is now and has to be now. You never know when your time will be up and your rental on your body suit will run its course. God forbid it happens, but you have to know that tomorrow is not promised. That individual that had a heart attack did not know this was going to happen. That individual who lost the battle to cancer did not know this was going to happen. For God, who sees and knows everything, knows your beginning as well as your ending.

We all must die one day, as this is a part of life. In understanding this, you have time now to determine what your legacy will be. As Steve Harvey once said, "The dash on your tombstone is what you will be remembered by." And with that being said, what will the dash on your tombstone say about you? Will you leave a legacy behind for your friends, family, and the world to see? Will you leave a mess for others to clean up? Will you say, "I wish I could have done this differently?"

      The way we live determines the way we will die. For instance, if you're dealing drugs and refuse to change, you're going to die in it. If you're killing folks, then don't be surprised when your number is called and revenge comes searching for you. If you're a man of God and live righteously, expect a victorious death. So as you can see, how we live will very well determine how we will die. The good news is that we don't have to die in our mess, but we can't be stubborn in determining when we will change. Today is your day and your time to change before it's too late. Who is it that you know that passed away before their time? It's many of children both young and older that have passed way too soon. Its many adults both young and old that have passed away too soon. These individuals did not know that they were going to die, which shows that we know not the minute or the hour of our last breath. But while you are still breathing, I encourage you to get things right with God before it's too late.

Everything that's going on around you clearly shows that we are in the last days. If you have not read Revelation, it's time, as this clearly represents what is going on in the world. Our world as we have known it has been subject to compromise. We compromise on gay marriages, we compromise on legalizing drugs, we compromise on police brutality, we compromise on getting involved with other countries that have nothing to do with us, and the list goes on. Things of the past that were unacceptable have now become acceptable. Our morals, standards, and ways of living have been relaxed, compromised, and accepted. The things of the world are not pleasing in the sight of God. And just because we are in the world does not mean we do not have to be of the world.

Somehow we got this notion that as a society it's okay to change and bend the rules to justify or satisfy others' wants and needs. And some churches are even compromising because they don't want their offering plates to get passed up. We have some men and women of God that compromise their ways in return for physical and material gain. Sometimes we as humans get so caught up in judging others and calling out others that we overlook ourselves. Nobody walking this earth is perfect, as we all fall short, and if we focused on ourselves first, our world would be a much better and happier place to live. For example, you can't judge a homosexual for being gay when you have a nasty lying spirit. How can you ever get through to them when they know you are a compulsive liar? And for all they know, you could be on the down-low. It's time to be real with ourselves and time to put our own self on blast. How can you tell a woman she's a hoe when you're an adulterer? Maybe if you set the example and prayed for her, then she could be delivered. Sometime folks are in the mess they are in because of us. How can someone get delivered when the folks that are in the leadership positions are the ringleaders? And the scary part is that it's not just in the world but also existing in the church.

We don't realize that we are accountable for folks as we may be the only form of Jesus that someone sees. If that was the case, what impression would you leave? Would you make Jesus out to be a drug dealer? Would you make Jesus out to be a man whore? Would you make Jesus out to be a pimp? Would you make Jesus out to be a murderer? If your sins were posted on the board for the world to see, how embarrassed would you be?

See, God forgave us so that we may live and not die, and we must understand that his forgiveness is in his salvation. Once we commit to God, he will commit to us, but with that being said, change has to take place. We can't say we are saved and have no desire to change. How can you be saved and still practice those same devilish behaviors with no desire to change? We are human, and our flesh is going to entice us, but there has to be a desire to be better and do better over time. Basically you should not still be sleeping around every night, as there should be some improvement taking place. Change does not happen overnight frequently, but there has to be an effort in the process.

And that effort says that, "I'm not one hundred percent delivered yet, but I'm better than I was and I'm presently working on it."

See, if we do the natural, God will add the super, and this gives us the supernatural. And in the supernatural those things that we were not strong enough to do alone now can be manifested because of God's presence in the matter. God's presence opens the door for mercy and grace to cover us when we don't deserve to be covered. In the Bible it says to love as this is the greatest commandment. If we as a nation tried loving one another instead of judging, how many terrorist attacks could we prevent? If we as a nation tried loving instead of judging, how many people would have skipped the going-to-jail process? If we as a nation tried loving instead of judging, how many prostitutes would change their ways? If we as a nation tried loving one another instead of judging, how many marriages would be saved and restored? If we as a nation tried loving one another instead of judging, how many deaths would be prevented? Instead of judging, we should love the hell out of them.

In the Bible it says love covers a multitude of things. This basically means, "I love you so much that I forgive you and don't hold your shortcomings against you." What if you truly loved someone so much that it made them change their ways? That's how God loves us, and God is love. And if we were created in God's image, why can we not represent God? How many lives could you save if you were a love representative?

Instead of selling sex, instead of selling stolen merchandise, instead of selling drugs, instead of selling your soul, why not give love? Since to give is to receive, if you give love, you will receive love back. Going a step further, if you reap what you sow, then if you sow love, you will reap love.

We as believers in the body of Christ must truly understand that only what you do for Christ will last. When you die, you can't take anything with you. You can be the richest man or woman in the world with all the accolades of the world, but when you die, you have nothing. The things of the world are only temporary, as one day the earth will pass away. Life is a blessing and should not be taken for granted. For those things you take for granted are those things you will surely loose. What is it that you are taking for granted today? If you truly knew that your tomorrow was not promised, you would not take life for granted.

It's funny how when we are in trouble, time is of the essence. A prime example is when I was small and I would get in trouble, I would run to God like I was running a marathon. In the process of running to God, I was expecting God to move immediately. And in every case, the trouble was because of my own doing. I would act out in school, and the teacher would call home or send a note. And my immediate instinct was to pray because I knew when I got home I was going to get whipped by mom. And I didn't know how to pray at this time, so I would say, "The Lord is my shepherd," over and over and over. This was my way of crying out to God for help and letting him know that I needed him right now and that time was not on my side.

In Psalms 27:5 it states, "For in the time of trouble He shall hide me in His pavilion; in the secret place of his tabernacle, he shall hide me; he shall set me high upon a rock." What if we put the same urgency in making now our time to put God first in our lives as we do when we are in trouble? When we are in court and facing life in prison or that lengthy sentence and we call on God, we expect a right-now move. When we are facing death on our hospital bed due to sickness, disease, illness, accident, or whatever the case may be, there is a right-now blessing needed. When we get caught stealing, lying, cheating, and our judgment has come full circle, we run to God without hesitation again needing a right-now blessing. When our back is against the wall and we are facing eviction, foreclosure, or repossession, and we need God to show up right now to block the initial outcome. We find ourselves in situations and circumstances whether saved or unsaved, and we ask God to save us before the time is up.

At some point in life, we have all done this or will do this, as we all run to God needing a right-now prayer whether directly or indirectly. In doing so, God hears us, and he answers us accordingly, but we must understand that our time is now with urgency. Our time to live right is now, our time to love right is now, our time to seek God is now, our time to forgive is now, our time to bask in his presence is now, our time to pray is now, etc. Our time, our time, our time, our time, our time, our time, our time, our time is now. What are you waiting for? What is it that you continue putting off that may not be so tomorrow? Are you going to church every Sunday saying, "I'll wait till next Sunday to get saved?" Are you holding that grudge saying, "I'll forgive when I get ready?" Are you not loving because you don't feel like they deserve it? If God did the same to you and treated you just as you treated others, would you be blessed or cursed? The same urgency that we come to God within our time of need is the same urgency we must use right now in seeking God. In doing so my friend, please don't put off today what is not promised tomorrow, as the time is now.

Chapter Five
Revelation and Destination

Lord let your revelation drive me to my destination, as this must be included in our daily prayer. First and foremost to understand your purpose here on earth, you must first understand Revelation. *Revelation* defined by Webster states it is "a usually secret or surprising fact that is made known; an act of making something known; an act of revealing something in usually a surprising way; something that surprises you; an act of revealing or communicating diving truth; something that is revealed by God to humans; an act of revealing to view or making known." In the New King James Version it states in Proverbs 29:18: "Where there is no revelation, the people cast off restraint; but happy is he who keeps the law."

In the Amplified Bible in Proverbs 29:18 it states, "Where there is no vision (no redemptive revelation of God), the people perish; but he who keeps the law (of God, which includes that of man)-blessed (happy, fortunate, and enviable) is he." In the New King James Version it states when the revelation is not present, people disregard restraint. This basically means if I don't have revelation, I don't have to obey the laws and follow rules. If I don't have revelation, I can't be trusted to make the right decisions. If you noticed, in the Amplified Bible vision and revelation are interchanged with one another. And basically this passage is stating that where the vision is absent, death is present. In other words, if you are lacking sight, your body will not function properly. This vision/sight is not ordinary eyesight but spiritual vision. This is seeing things in God's eyes, which I call kingdom vision. So in other words, your vision, or revelation, can determine whether you live or die.

In the New King James Version Bible in Revelation 1:1 it states, "The Revelation of Jesus Christ, which God gave Him to show His servants-things which must shortly take place." Again in the New King James Version it reveals that through revelation, people are able to see things that will soon take place. These individuals are not limited to but can be Apostles, Bishops, Pastors, Prophets, Elders, Evangelists, visionaries, dreamers, men and women of God, children, and the list goes on. God can use these individuals to give warnings of good and bad things that are set to come to pass.

In the Amplified Bible in Revelation 1:1 it states, "This is the revelation of Jesus Christ (His unveiling of the divine mysteries). God gave it to Him to disclose and make known to his bond servants certain things which must shortly and speedily come to pass in their entirety." In the Amplified Bible it shows Jesus is sharing with us divine mysteries given by the Father, who knows all and sees all, prior to these things coming to pass. In the book of Revelation in particular, among other books, it reveals the unveiling of the last days. Not only does it reveal specifics, but it tells of events that will come to pass and how things will change. For example, it talks of how everything will be computerized and chips will be inserted. And in today's society all of our credit cards have chips inserted in them. It also speaks of war which is in the making, as you see all of these countries in disputes with one another.

In the Bible the last book is called Revelation, and if you notice, this book reveals things that are to come to pass. In the Webster's dictionary, as well as the Bible, they both confirm revelations are those things to be revealed by God. If you have not read Revelation, this is a must read, as it will scare the hell out of you for those not saved so you won't have to settle for the mark of the beast and be damned eternally. By utilizing this revelation that God has made available to us, we can save our souls from going to hell. For example, if you have a dream that you are going to die, take it to heart, as this could be a warning sign that something is trying to take you out. Don't be afraid or scared but be wise and fight death with life. You do this by getting your life in order with God and then reverse the revelation. God has given us the authority to speak life to our situations by speaking those things that be not as though they were. For death, Father, you have given me life; for lack, Father, you have given me abundance. For you are the righteousness of God; and I am in right standing with God. The power of life and death is in your mouth, but you have to know this. What you say can make or break those deadly situations that the enemy has put in place to take you out.

Now that we got a clear understanding of revelation, we can experience our destination. "Lord, let me arrive at my destination in my due season through your revelation" is what we should also be praying every day. We were all put here for a reason at birth, and this reason can also be seen as our destination. God has a purpose for each and every individual on the face of this earth. God has an appointed time for us to operate in this purpose (gift), which again is our destination. Webster defines *destination* as "a place to which a person is going or something is being sent; the purpose for which something is destined; an act of appointing, setting aside for a purpose, or predetermining; a place to which one is journeying or to which something is sent." In the New King James Version in Lamentations 1:9 it states, "Her uncleanness is in her skirts; she did not consider her destiny; Therefore her collapse was awesome; she had no comforter." In this particular passage it shows that every destination does not have a happy ending; in fact, it can take you to destruction. Because of her unwillingness to change and hardened heart, she overlooked God's plan for her and took a detour seeking her own selfishness over God's commandments.

In the Bible it says, "Seek the kingdom first, and then destiny can be added." If you don't seek God and follow his commandments, then your death will be great. In the Amplified Bible, Lamentations 1:9 states, "Her filthiness was in and on her skirts; she did not (seriously and earnestly) consider her final end. Therefore she has come down (from throne to slavery) singularly and astonishingly; she has no comforter." In this passage it shows the disgust God has in her disobedience, which should be a wake-up call for us. When we don't consider God, then he doesn't consider us.

For instance, when we are out in the streets selling those drugs and given warning after warning with blatant disregard of the Holy Spirit, our consequences become great, as prison and death are looking for us. When we are prostituting our bodies and disregard the voice of the Lord, our consequences become great, as disease and death are looking for us. When we are out stealing and making this our profession and disregard our Father, prison and death are looking for us. When we are out abusing and murdering individuals without disregard, death and prison are looking for us. When we are out raping and molesting individuals without any regard, God sees it and is not pleased, as prison and death are looking for us. It doesn't matter how big or how small the sin is. Know that God is not pleased, and it will eventually lead to destruction.

We have to take heed in the body of Christ and truly understand we were put here for a purpose that goes far beyond our own selfish wants and desires. So what is it that you need to work on that is detouring your destination? Is it that backbiting spirit that got you compromising? Is it that gossiping spirit that got you comprising? Is it that adulterous spirit that got you compromising? Is it that lying spirit that got you compromising?

Is it that disobedient spirit that got you compromising? Is it that murderous spirit that got you compromising? Is it that thieving spirit that got you compromising? Is it that lusting spirit that got you compromising? Is it that witchcraft spirit that got you compromising? Is it that pornography spirit that got you compromising? What is it that you are allowing to separate you from destination?

    God has destined all of us to be great at our gift, but if we are not in his will, we will never see his promises for us. It's like when your parents make a will for their children and they put stipulations on the inheritance. The stipulation could be you have to be married, you have to graduate from high school, you have to graduate from college, and the list goes on. This is what God does for us as well; he puts stipulations on his promises for us because he loves us that much. God's stipulations are that we are saved, living for him, and staying in his will. This just basically means that you seek after God's righteousness and that you are in right standing with God. That is why your destination is for an appointed time because if you get it too soon, you might be wasteful. For instance, if God gives a drug addict millions, what do you think will happen with the money? If God gives a whoremonger millions, what do you think will happen with the money? If God gives a thief millions, what do you think will happen with the money? If God gives a drug dealer millions, what do you think would happen with the money? God will never bless you in your mess, as he loves you that much and is not willing to pay for your ticket to hell.

Now that we've discussed both revelation and destination, we can add the two together. When you add revelation to destination, you get prosperity, blessings, favor, increase, wisdom, and strength. So because of your revelation, you are able to reach your destination. Revelation may reveal that it's not your time now, but you have to be wise and patient enough to receive this. Revelation may send you in an opposite direction or to a new course which could speed up your destination. Again you have to be open to receive revelation whether it be from your pastor, official man or woman of God, prophet, or God himself. Every revelation you get will not always be good news, but you have to accept the bad and be obedient to the Word just as you would to good news. For example, God could give you a revelation that if you marry a certain individual, you will die. You have to get out of the natural and into the spiritual, as discernment will give you understanding and wisdom as to how to proceed. Revelation can also be perceived as a warning, as it was in this particular instance. In your obedience, you will reach your desired destination. That individual God warned you not to marry could have been a cold-blooded murderer and you never knew it.

You cannot reach your destination without guidance, wisdom, knowledge, and obedience. When God speaks, you better listen, as it's for your own good. Every great leader in the

Bible reached their destination through God's revelation. Take Noah; he had to listen to God to know how to build the ark, when to leave, what to take, etc. If Noah had disobeyed, what would have been the outcome? Take Moses; he had to listen to God to know how to free his people after a long, hard-fought process. If Moses had disobeyed God, what would have been the outcome? This is just a few of many great leaders in the Bible who had to solely trust, rely, and depend on God for revelation to reach their destination. In doing so, not every day was easy, pleasant, or fun, but God saw them through. Sometimes we get off track, and God has to give us a wake-up call to get us back where we need to be. Take Jonah; God gave him specific instructions, when he disobeyed he was swallowed by a whale. What if God had let him die in his mess? Repent from your wicked ways, ask God for revelation, and go in peace to your destination.

Chapter Six
Covering

In life there are many things we need for survival, such as food, oxygen, water, and clothes. These are all considered to be necessities and impossible to live without. Well, this list is missing covering, as we all need to be covered by a spiritual parent. This covering can only be found in a designated church home. A spiritual parent can consist of a spiritual dad, spiritual mom, or both. A spiritual parent is your parent in the spiritual realm, as they cover you spiritually just as a parent would do naturally. From a natural standpoint mom and dad are your natural parents. Mom and dad's job is to cover you, protect you, guide you, keep you safe, and teach you. They ultimately raise you from a child to an adult. And what they put in you determines what comes out of you in most cases.

In the Bible it says train a child up so they may grow and not depart from you. This is where your spiritual parents come in. While your parents teach you from a natural standpoint, your spiritual parents' job is to teach you how to live righteously and grow in God. The entire purpose of a covering is to help keep and sustain your salvation through accountability. This basically means when you're going through tough times, you have someone praying for you. And when you're going through good times, you have someone celebrating with you. The same way your parents show you how to live, your spiritual parents do the same, as they're your first example as to how your life should look from a spiritual living standpoint.

Salvation is not an easy road, as it is a challenge to stay saved. It takes dedication, discipline, and determination to stay consistent in living a well balanced Christian life. You have to be dedicated in your walk refusing to go back to your previous ways. You have to have discipline to resist temptation of the enemy. You have to have determination in order to stay on this road and stay the course at all costs.

In living right, you begin to change your way of thinking, and your desires change during this process. The things you used to do, you no longer have the same desire as you once had before. As a child of God with a covering, you become kingdom-minded and Christ-like. When you walk and talk, you are a representative of Christ and are charged to walk in his ways. As a spiritual son or daughter you take on the identity of your spiritual parents. With that being said you have to be really selective in choosing your covering. When you're born, you cannot choose your natural parents; however, when you become saved and make a decision to live for God, you can choose your spiritual parents. Your spiritual parents should resemble God and be your first example of kingdom living. If this is not the case, then you have to seek God to help you find the right spiritual parents.

And you should never choose spiritual parents out of obligation. This basically means that if your natural family has a church, you should never go join or become a member because of your family's attendance. This can be a spiritual hindrance if you go to church for anything outside of seeking God for yourself. If your brother or sister has a church, it's okay to support them and attend the church. But if you always see them as a brother or sister versus your pastor or a representative of God, then it will be hard for you to hear and know God's voice. And although you love your family members and want to support them, never sacrifice your soul. This is not saying you cannot serve under your family, because sometimes this can be the best place for you. This is more of an intelligence and understanding concept, as you have to use wisdom in this situation and seek God for direction.

  In the Bible it says anyone seeking wisdom let him ask God for wisdom. If you do not seek God for wisdom regarding your spiritual parents, you could struggle as it relates to spiritual growth. We go to church for fellowship, to grow in spirit, to grow in truth, and to gain understanding of the only true and living God. If you are in church for any other reason, then you are dead wrong. We are all guilty of this at times, as I can admit growing up I was in church as a teenager seeking females. And because of this, my spirit was not fed and the enemy used me as a vessel of distraction to hinder others that were there seeking God's face. Because I was not in tune with God, I was a hindrance and distraction to others who were actually there not due to situation, or circumstance, but because of want and desire.

And with that being said, you have to use wisdom, as only you know if that spiritual man and woman of God is for you.

The way you can tell if you are at the right church and under the proper covering is through your walk with God. Do you desire to be better? Are you growing spiritually? Are you saved, sanctified, and full of the Holy Ghost? Are you seeking God's face versus your own agenda? Is your will lining up to God's will for you? Are you still in the world? When you fall short or mess up, do you immediately repent? When the man or woman of God brings forth the Word, are you able to receive the Word with the ability to execute? Does God reside in you? Are you a representation of the church when you are in the world? Do you love as Christ loves? Are you a hearer and doer of the Word? These are all questions that will reflect if your decision is the correct one.

Obligation will never lead you on the right path; you have to follow your heart and most importantly God on all circumstances. This decision cannot be taken lightly, as this is one of the most important decisions you could ever make in life. It may not seem like it's that big of a deal, but it's actually larger than life. Your decision can determine if you go to heaven or hell, which is basically saying it can make a difference as to where you reside in eternity. God said he is the way, the truth, and the light, and as men and women of God we have to get into his presence to experience him personally. If your man or woman of God cannot get you there or speak into your life regarding your situations, you may not be in the right church.

Not every church is for everyone; a church that fits you may not fit your mom, dad, cousin, uncle, brother, sister, friend, etc., and vice versa. Your circumstances may call for a teacher versus a hooper or hollier. And in many circumstances you may be looking for that spiritual parent who has been through that unique circumstance that you've been going through so they can help you defeat the test that's been holding you back. For example, if you haven't been raped, it will be hard for you to tell someone how to get through being raped. If you haven't had cancer, it will be hard for you to tell that individual how to make it when you're losing all of your hair and your body is all out of whack. If you haven't been abused as a child, it will be hard for you to tell someone how to handle abuse. If you hadn't been lied to or cheated on, it will be hard to tell someone how to handle the situation. If you haven't been shot or stabbed, it will be hard to tell someone how to get over this situation. If you haven't been a fornicator or prostitute, it will be hard to tell someone how to change their circumstances.

Spiritual parents have been handpicked by God and are ordained and graced for certain individuals. God does not always use those individuals who haven't had any challenges in life and haven't been through hell and back. But God likes to use those individuals who were completely messed up, strung out on dope, alcoholics, murderers, liars, cheaters, drug dealers, and just overall bad people. See by doing this, it assures the world that this could have been nothing but God. Everyone has that one challenged individual in your family or a friend of the family. And this particular individual is a partygoer, drinker, smoker, fornicator, etc. and openly lives for the world with no regard for God. God likes those individuals because when God saves that individual and cleans them up, there is no doubt that it could have been no one but God. God takes the scumbags, the dirty folks, the drug addicts, the alcoholics, and those individuals who have no passion or desire for life. When God creates in them a clean heart and changes their way of thinking, those individuals become on fire for God. They are walking, talking, Holy Ghost-filled, spirit-speaking prayer warriors, mighty men and women of God.

      You take Saul; Saul was a murderer who was only out to kill Christians who were preaching and spreading the Word of God. Saul was feared by many and was bold in his worldly life. When God got a hold of Saul, not only did he save him, but he changed his name in addition to his entire way of thinking. God blinded Saul to get his attention and let Saul know he was not pleased with his murderous ways, in what he was doing. God took the very person who was of the world and used him to preach the gospel and bring others to the Lord. Through Saul's testimony, he was able to reach those individuals who had been broken. If God can take a cold-blooded killer and change him into a power-packed preacher, what can't he do? If God can take a wretch like me and give me a desire to live right, what can't he do? God uses our spiritual parents mightily, as he assigns us to our parents and they are held accountable for our salvation. So when you think about making that bad decision, think about that spiritual mom or dad that stayed up all night praying for you. Think about how that spiritual mom or dad would feel if you robbed that bank, stole from the job, committed adultery, sold that weed, smoked that crack, molested that little boy or girl, fornicated with those church members, and the list goes on.

By having a covering and being under the right spiritual parents, you are able to grow spiritually in God. Your faith becomes great, and those things you speak will be produced on earth. Even in the Bible God spoke to leaders and used those leaders to speak to the people. Noah was one of those leaders of his time. God spoke to Noah as to how the destruction would be carried out and what he needed to do to survive the flood. Moses was another one of those great leaders of his time. God spoke to Moses as to how he would deliver the children of Israel. If the people walked away and did not follow their spiritual leader, how much different could things have been? If the children of Israel were disobedient, they would not have ever made it out of slavery and been delivered from the hands of pharaoh. Sometimes the answer to that problem that you are seeking a solution for is in your leader's mouth. And if you are not obedient and willing to hearken to the voice of the Lord, then you will miss the move.

On the other end of that, if you don't have a leader to follow, you won't have anyone to speak into your life or clear direction for the journey. Every great leader has a spiritual leader who they can go to for guidance and understanding. One of the best things about a spiritual parent is they won't always tell you what you want to here or agree with what you say but they will follow God's command in every given situation. If you don't have a covering, please seek God and ask him to show you where to go, as your life depends on it. Your spiritual mom, spiritual dad, or both will always want to see you do good as they are invested in you. While the natural is good, sometimes you have to get out of the natural and tap into the spiritual realm. And by tapping into the spiritual realm, you begin to unlock some things in the natural. And more importantly, you also begin to see God's will for your life through those speaking into your life assigned by God. Now that you know, never go another day without being covered, for God loves you and I do too.

Chapter 7
Create in Me a Clean Heart

When we openly accept Jesus Christ into our hearts as our Lord and Savior, we should be saying to God, create in me a clean heart. With salvation comes change, meaning we deviate from our old ways. The things we used to do, we no longer have the same desires to do those things anymore. When we accept God, we divorce the devil, and all of our old ways pass away as new ways begin. It's like saying, "I used to be a drug dealer, but I no longer desire to be the dope man anymore." It's like saying, "I used to run a prostitution ring, but I no longer desire to sell sex for monetary gain." It's like saying, "I used to abuse my children, but I no longer desire to take out my anger and frustrations on my children anymore." It's like saying, "I used to listen to and embrace negativity, but I no longer desire to submit to the enemy." It's like saying, "I used to worship other gods and live for Satan, but I no longer desire to choose death over life." It's like saying, "I used to steal and be like a thief in the night, but I no longer desire to continue on this path of destruction."

By accepting salvation, you are acknowledging that Jesus is Lord and asking him to come into your heart. For those not saved, it's as simple as saying, "Father, you are the Christ, son of the living God, I believe you died for me and rose on the third day, forgive me for all of my sins. I've done wrong, but right now I change loyal ships, I make Jesus Christ Lord and

Savior of my life; therefore, I am saved." It's that simple; by saying this, you are telling God that you believe he died for your sins and you invite him to come into your heart. You must be sincere in your request, as God will not dwell in an unclean temple. If there is no seriousness or sincerity in your confession, then you're better off not saying it. However, if you have a true desire to change and want God to do a new thing in you, then you must first confess with your mouth that he is Lord. By making this first step of confession, you give God access to your heart.

Once you ask God to come into your heart, he has to wash, clean, and purge all of those past things that were dwelling in your body. That fornication demon has to go, that lust demon has to go, that lying demon has to go, that bisexual demon has to go, that lesbian demon has to go, that suicidal demon has to go, that cancerous demon has to go, that negativity demon has to go, that backbiting demon has to go, that stealing demon has to go, that poverty demon has to go, that lack demon has to go, that hot-tempered demon has to go, that hatred demon has to go, that unfaithful demon has to go, that molestation demon has to go, that pornography demon has to go, that serving-other-gods demon has to go, and any other demons that's dwelling in you must go.

When you pray to God, ask him to create in you a clean heart. We as humans are flesh and blood, and we battle against rulers and principalities. This basically means that even though we get saved, we will still get tested in those areas we struggled in. The enemy comes to steal, kill, and destroy, meaning he does not like you, and he wants to take you out. With that being said, when you are saved, your salvation will be tested. The enemy will always attack your weaknesses and expose your sin. For instance, if you were an alcoholic, the enemy will have someone bring your favorite drinks to you free of charge. If you were a fornicator, the enemy will bring the men or women to you. If you were a junkie, the enemy will provide the drugs for you to kill yourself. When you sin, you have to repent immediately because the enemy will try and make you feel like you're nothing once you get saved and fall short. He'll tell you things like you're not saved, you went back to your old ways, you don't have to live right, it's okay, you're not perfect, do it again, and so on.

      You have to know who you are and whose you are, and with that being said, you have to be quick to repent. If you are quick to sin, you should be even quicker to repent. Even when you get saved, you will fall, but you must not wait to get up. In the Bible it says we have all sinned and come short of the glory of God. This simply means that we are not perfect and will miss the mark; however, even though we miss the mark, we have to try and avoid the same pitfalls. If you accidentally make a bad move, you have to first repent and then take yourself out of that situation. For instance, if you're shacking up and you're having a hard time not fornicating, you have to look at your situation. You have to put yourself in a position to be successful, so in this particular incident, somebody needs to move out or there should be a wedding taking place immediately in the event that both parties are ready and in agreement.

    The good thing about salvation is when you're in the wrong, you are convicted. Being convicted is basically God letting you know that you're doing something wrong and that he's not pleased with your actions. Conviction can also be seen as restriction. When God convicts you of something it's almost like he's restricting you from something. For instance, if you are fornicating, God will convict you, letting you know that's not right. Once you repent with sincerity and ask God to help you, then he will aid you in the restriction part of it. In your sincerity and prayer request for help, God will eliminate the ease of fornication. When you ask God to create in you a clean heart, you ask God to change your heart. When you ask God to change your heart, it's like a 360, or complete turnaround. It's almost like you're going from hot to cold and vice versa. You'll go from being a beggar and a thief to a giver and a lover. Please be mindful that this does not happen overnight but it's a process.

    In the King James Bible in 1 Samuel 16:7 it says: "But the Lord said to Samuel, 'Do not look at his appearance or at his physical stature, because I have refused him. For the Lord does not see as man sees; for man looks at the outward appearance, but the Lord looks at the heart." This clearly shows how God sees us, not from our outward appearance but from what's inside. What if we see people for what's inside versus always looking at the outside first? If God judges us by our heart, why are we judging by outward appearances? For those of us that are all that and a bag of chips, you haven't always been all of that. You haven't always had your hair, nails, and feet done. You haven't always had those fancy handbags and red bottoms. You haven't always had that Louis Vuitton and Versace. You haven't always had that black card with unlimited access to money. You haven't always had that Bugatti, Rolls-Royce, and Maybach. You haven't always had that Rolex, Movado, and Rafael Nadal. You haven't always had that yacht, private jet, and house on the hills. In fact, before you acquired all of these items, you ate Oodles and Noodles. Before you acquired all these things, you rode the bus. Before you acquired all these things, you were robbing Peter to pay Paul. And for those born into money, your family was not always rich; just go back some generations ago.

    I say that to say materials does not make a person; it's what's inside. God does not care about your materials, and the same way you acquired them, you can easily lose them. If you haven't heard it before, then I'll share with you what the bible says regarding this. The Bible says the wealth of the wicked is stored up for the just. This basically means that if you're acquiring wealth by the wrong means, you're wasting time. The wrong way defined means illegal, disapproved by God, stealing involved, hurting or harming others, and anything that has a consequence behind the action. So if this is you, time to repent and change your ways, or otherwise, you're just building a wealth pool for a saint patiently waiting to receive their wealth transfer. Our God, who knows all and sees all, rewards faithfulness, and if we are faithful to God, then he is faithful to us, and all answers to our prayers are ye and amen. Also be mindful that what you sow is what you will reap. If you sow bad things, then you will reap bad things. If your attitude is bad, than you will attract others with bad attitudes.

However, on the other side, if you sow love and generosity, you will reap love and generosity. In the King James Bible in Psalms 51:10 it says: "Create in me a clean heart, O God, And renew a steadfast spirit within me." When we seek God and his presence and ask him to create a clean heart in us, he cleanses us of all unrighteousness. And if you notice, it also states, "Renew a steadfast spirit in me." This is basically saying, "Preserve me, Lord. Help me to stay saved, take out everything in me that does not please you, strengthen me in your Word, use me for your will and your way, help me to live right, help me to make the right decisions, let my life be pleasing to you, Lord, and let your glory shine brightly upon me."

It is very important that you truly understand what you are asking when you ask God to create a clean heart in you. It's almost like rebuilding a house that has been set on fire. First, you have to gut out everything in the house. If you're rebuilding the house to be new, then you must first eliminate all of the old stuff. And considering that a fire took place, you can't build something new with damaged goods. Once you take everything old out of the house, then you begin to rebuild the house. In the rebuilding process, all of the old items that were removed must now be replaced by new items. In building a house, you must ensure you have a solid foundation, as this is what keeps the house intact and protects it from wicked weather. Once the foundation is in place and you have put all new items in the house, then the moving-in process begins. The same takes place in us when we accept God in our lives. In order for God to reside in us, we must first die or catch on fire. This simply means everything that's in us must come out. And some of the stuff in us must be burned out and buried in the sea of forgetfulness. We have to get torn down just as the house gets torn down. Then we must be gutted out just as the house is gutted out.

Our foundation then must be reestablished. In re-establishing our foundation, we have to be rooted and planted in God. To be rooted and planted in God is to be rooted and planted in the Word. We build our relationship with God through his Word. In the Gospel of John it states: "In the beginning was the Word and the Word was with God, and the Word was God." This basically states that the Word was here with God before the world was established. Going a step further, everything in the world, including us, is a product of the Word. For example, God said, "Let there be light," and light appeared. God created the earth through words, so everything in the earth is a product of a word. So once we are rooted in the Word, then we have a solid foundation and God can begin to furnish our home. God can only furnish our home after we accept God into our heart as our Lord and Savior. God can only furnish our home after he creates in us a clean heart. God can only furnish our home after we make the decision to die to the world.

Once we make the decision to divorce the world and turn from our wicked ways, then God can unleash his promises that he gave to our fathers and forefathers. And when God furnishes your home, there's nothing average about your home. In my father's house, there are many mansions, so if my father has many mansions, then what shall I have? If the streets of heaven are paved in gold and I'm a joint heir to my father's house, then how much more will my inheritance be? When making a decision between the club and church, just ask yourself, do I want deceiving temporary pleasure, or do I want everlasting joy that the world can't take and the world can't give? It's as simple as saying, "Lord, create in me a clean heart."

Chapter Eight
Creative Arts

In the King James Bible in the book of Ephesians 2:10 it states, "For we are His workmanship, created in Christ Jesus for good works, which God prepared beforehand that we should walk in them." This shows how we are simply products of God, as he created us in his own image. We were created for good works which God predestined beforehand that we should walk in his ways. Another way of looking at this word *workmanship* is we are God's handiwork, we are God's creation, and we are God's mini me's. First you notice, it states we are created in Christ Jesus for good works, as we miss this part quite frequently. The Word does not say we were created to sin. This word does not say we were created to backbite. This word does not say we were created to kill. This word does not say we were created to steal. This word does not say we were created to lust. This word does not say we were created to fornicate. This word does not say we were created to prophalie. This word does not say we were created to commit adultery. This word does not say we were created to gossip. This word does not say that we were created to cheat. This word does not say that we were created to be abusive. This word does not say that we were created to serve the enemy. This word does not say that we were created to be deceitful. This word does not say that we were created to shack up. This word does not say that we were created to for selfishness. This word does not say that we were created to serve other gods. This word does not say that we were created to doubt. This word does not say that we were created to worry. And the list goes on and on, as this word simply says we were created for good works.

What is that work in you that needs to be birthed out? After this, it states "God has created these good works through Christ Jesus beforehand." So before we were born God gave us all a gift. This is confirmation that you are greater than your present life may reflect. Your greatness was established in you by God before you came out of your mother's womb, before you took your first breath, and before you ever opened your eyes for the first time. So with that being said, what gift is buried down inside of you that the world is waiting for? What is that one thing you can do all day that you never get tired of? What is that one thing you have been graced to do? What is that one thing you do better than anyone else? Once you truly tap into this gift, then you will experience and become a witness of the true glory of God in your life. Until you engage in your gift, you cannot be about your father's business. Your nine-to-five that you work every day is probably not your gift. It's time to reflect on where you are in life and ask God to show you how to operate in your gift.

The gift that God has given cannot be stopped, denied, or blocked by man. God has given you this gift for such a time as now. For tomorrow is not promised to anyone and today will one day pass away which simply means you don't have time to wait; it's time to walk into your destiny. Prepare yourself for greatness and give your all to God so he can share the gifts in you with the world. We all have creative works that were placed in us at birth. Some people leave this earth without ever allowing their creative works to surface. The world that we are living in is so corrupt if we don't make ourselves part of the solution then ultimately we are part of the problem. Let go and let God use you; never be afraid to walk with God as he is the only way.

Mom, dad, sister, brother, cousin, uncle, aunt, grandma, granddad, friend, guardian, BFF, coworker, boss, Satan himself, and anyone else in your life does not have a heaven or hell to put you in. Never let people who have no control on this earth control your destiny and outcome. Everyone walking the face of the earth is human, as we are all equal and created in God's image. One day we will all have to stand before God when our time is up. When that day comes, will he say, "Well done, my good and faithful servant?" Or will he say, "Depart from me, I never knew you?" Will you choose life or death? Will you choose heaven or hell? Will you choose to live for people, or will you choose to live for God? Will you choose creative works or life's circumstances and situations? Time's up; time to make a decision. I choose creative works starting now until eternity. Don't believe me; just watch!

Greeting Card: Greetings for God

Open up your mouth
    And let your heart be exposed
        To the greatness of his glory
            Which can only be received in salvation
                Let go and let God live in you on today

Won't you let me usher you in

To the presence of God

Where his glory is present

And he washes you of sin

Grace and Mercy has kept you thus far

But the time has come for you to be who God says you are

Won't you start by just saying these simple words

God forgive me for I have sinned

Come into my heart so my life can begin

I believe you died for a wretch like me

And on this day I'm ready to be who you called me to be!

I love you my friend and welcome you in the kingdom!

        Greetings for God
        By: Luther T. Collins
        Coming Soon

Thy Kingdom First "About My Father's Business"
Contents Poem

Salvation is everything, for without God we are nothing.
First we confess; then we get blessed, and watch God do the rest.

Habakkuk 2:2, God said write the vision and make it plain.
When you get tired of going through, you'll expose the sunshine
    and eliminate the rain.

Grace and Mercy shall set me free when I'm in my mess.
Little do I know it's running out, and my testimony may never
    be birthed if I don't pass this test.

The time is now, for we are living in the last days.
When your story is told, will there be a lasting legacy for others
    to read about or a bunch of blank pages?

Revelation will drive you to your destination.
But if you never seek God, your driver's-seat experience will
    always be speculation.

Covering can only be experienced when you join a ministry.
Choose wisely, as your spiritual parents are your stairway to the
    heaven or ski slope to hell.

Create in me a clean heart, nameless and blameless, that will uplift my soul.
For I wanna see my loved ones and walk the streets paved in gold.

Creative arts says, what will your legacy say about you?
Will you be a fool stuck in the world, or will your gift be exposed by letting God use you?

Thy Kingdom First "About My Father's Business" Spoken Word Piece

I'm about my father's business in this historic year
I will boldly proclaim glory over my life without fear
Satan, you're a liar, and I won't allow you to be in my ear

Every obstacle, every circumstance is just an opportunity for victory
God's already done it, and there's just no stopping me
I was once lost, but now I see it's nothing but his glory

All because I seek ye the kingdom first
And put my life in proper kingdom order to defeat the family curse
God, family, work as this is not scripted for there is no time to rehearse

God did it all because I submitted my soul to his ways
Now because of this in my heart his presence forever stays
I'm a Christian; it's what I do and definitely not a phase

And because I put God first, I'm blessed beyond what eyes can see
I am everything that I am only because of God's grace and his mercy
I fall short, but I get up quickly in my authority because I know who I be

Not just a mere man in a body but a royal priest of the most high
I don't have to see him, because he's shining down on me from the sky
If you ever want to experience life like never before, then give God a try

Kingdom minded, kingdom living, kingdom glory
Who is it that can be against me when God is for me
I live in assurance of life, as this concludes my story

About My Father's Business
Gospel Hip Hop Track

The business of the matter
Is the business at hand
If you don't rock with me,
Then you won't understand
About his business
Yeah, yeah
About his business
Yeah, yeah
(Repeat)

I got sixteen bars, only sixteen bars
For all the pain and the scars
Yet I still go to war
All this hell on earth
Through defeat of these trials, it's all on my chest
The snares of the enemy will not let me rest
But no matter how it looks
But no matter how it seems
I still trust and believe
By faith I receive
All my blessings hundred fold
'Cause my God oh-so-cold
He said - keep my kingdom first

Let it be known in this verse
I ride or die for my Savior
Now check out my royal flavor

The business of the matter
Is the business at hand
If you don't rock with me,
Then you won't understand
About his business
Yeah, yeah
About his business
Yeah, yeah
(Repeat)

About My Father's Business
Stage Play

Scene 1

SNOOPY: Dad, Peanut ain't take out the trash yesterday!

PEANUT: STOP SNITCHING and get your peanut-butter-and-jelly-eating self *(making a peanut butter and jelly sandwich)* up out my mom's kitchen.

SNOOPY: Whatever, but you know Dad gone get you, right?

PEANUT: You shut up before I get you *(walking in Snoopy's direction)*.

SNOOPY: *(calls dad while leaving out the kitchen door)* Dad, Daddy, Dad, Daddy, Dad, Daddy *(Daddy Ross gives him a long, hard stare as they pass each other walking in and out of the kitchen)*.

DADDY ROSS: *(comes barging in the kitchen)* What in the Sam Sausage Head is going on now?

SNOOPY: *(turns and comes back in the kitchen)* Peanut ain't doing his part to keep the castle clean?

PEANUT: What castle? I don't see no castle to keep clean.

DADDY ROSS: Boy, how many times I gotta tell you? You have to be about your Father's business. Don't you know our Father in heaven gives us according to our faith and based on if we are good stewards of what he's already given us?

PEANUT: Pop, I just don't know why you always comin' at me like I'm one of those lost souls you minister to on the street. I'm not that guy, I tell you, so stop trying to get me to be like you. I'm no preacher man.

DADDY ROSS: I don't want you to be like me, Son, but I also don't want you to burn in hell for your stubbornness for eternity either. Boy, you better take off them gasoline draws before you catch a fire.

PEANUT: Pop, no disrespect, but the only thing that's gone catch a fire is your breath. Mama done told you to stop eating them hot Cheetos for breakfast. I'm surprised your butt ain't burning.

DADDY ROSS: Okay, Peanut, just remember you were the disobedient sheep that strayed from his shepherd. God is not pleased with what you're doing and he is trying to get your attention. I won't be here forever, you know. One day you'll look for me, and I'll be gone.

PEANUT: Good, maybe you'll stop lecturing me then.

DADDY ROSS: You know what, boy (*looking at his son, shaking his head in displeasure*), one day you'll understand. Until you put the kingdom first and be about your Father's business, things will never work out in life for you. Now go take out that trash and do something constructive with yourself.

PEANUT: *takes out trash bag*

Lights Dim

End of Scene 1

Scene 2

SNOOPY: (*Walks in the house and sees Peanut on the couch*): Pop gone, Bruh (*Snoopy says with a really long and convincing face*).

PEANUT: *(Crying out loud in anger and rage while fighting the air)* OH, WHY ME, OH LORD! Why you had to take my daddy? He was all I had, and you took him away!

SNOOPY: Peanut, you all right, bro (*Embraces his big brother*)? You gotta be strong for the family.

PEANUT: Be strong for the family? What about me? He was my daddy, and God took him away from me.

SNOOPY: He was my daddy too, and I love him just as much as you.

PEANUT: You sure got one helluva way of showing it!

SNOOPY: Oh my bag, I guess I should be fighting the air with you too (*Starts swinging to fight the air with Peanut*). Watch out for the guy behind you (*Swings behind Peanut*)! I got'em, big bro. He almost took you outta here.

PEANUT: Very funny, man, ain't got time for your shenanigans right now.

SNOOPY: Good, 'cause I ain't got time for yours either. Daddy warned you that he wasn't gonna be around much longer, just like he warned me. You didn't listen to him, and you didn't listen to God.

PEANUT: All he kept saying was be about your Father's Business, whatever that is supposed to mean.

SNOOPY: That means that you have to hearken to the voice of your heavenly Father, who sees all and knows all. Pop knew he was leaving, as his blood pressure was out of control for some time now. I'm just grateful that he passed in his sleep, no more pain, no more suffering.

PEANUT: I guess you right, Little Bro, but why now and why our dad?

SNOOPY: Truth be told, God revealed to me in a dream that in order for you to live, Daddy must die. That is the only way God could get your attention. Sometimes he has to take you so low that he is the only person that can pull you out. And when you come out of that place, you will know it was nobody but God that brought you out.

PEANUT: So what do I do from here?

SNOOPY: First and foremost, you confess with your mouth that Jesus is Lord and Savior of your life and ask him to forgive you of your sins.

PEANUT: (*Prays a salvation prayer*) Done. What's next?

SNOOPY: Then you seek God like never before and study his Word. You must put God first in all that you do, as he honors the prayers of the righteous.

PEANUT: I got it (Begins to pray God will bring his dad back).

DADDY ROSS: *(walks in the back door)* Hey, what's up, Sons? The fishing trip was the bomb. Thank you guys for the new boat.

PEANUT: What (Turns and looks at Snoopy with a pissed-off look)! Boy, you lied to me. I ought to beat the breaks off of you. Dead people don't fish.

SNOOPY: Remember, Big Bro, you just got saved now.

PEANUT: Dad, what's up? Y'all playing tricks on me now?

DADDY ROSS: Sorry, Son, I won't lose another child to the enemy. I love you too much for that. Besides ain't you glad I'm still alive amongst the living?

PEANUT: Yeah, Dad, you got me, and I know, be about my father's business.

DADDY ROSS: So proud of you, Son. Now pray us out!

PEANUT: *Says a prayer for the close out.*

The End

Until The Next Chapter

Thank you all so much for purchasing my book, I hope it has been a blessing to you as it has been to me in writing. This is one of the few times that I get to share a wide variety of the many gifts to the world that God has blessed me with. God has truly graced me and anointed my hands in writing for such a critical time as this. Please feel free to share this book with your family, friends, coworkers, and anyone in need of encouragement. Life is not always easy, as we all experience peaks and valleys during different stages of our lives. Sometimes God puts people in our lives for certain seasons to help us through those tough times. When you come out of the season, please go back and help others who are coming behind you. I'm so grateful that God chose me for such a time as this. I love you all and hope you will continue to follow and support me in my future endeavors as the best is yet to come.

Your Friend For Life,

Luther T. Collins

www.ingramcontent.com/pod-product-compliance
Lightning Source LLC
Chambersburg PA
CBHW071027080526
44587CB00015B/2527